PRO-SYSTEMS

COMPLETE STRAIGHT BATON MANUAL
FOR POLICE & SECURITY OFFICERS

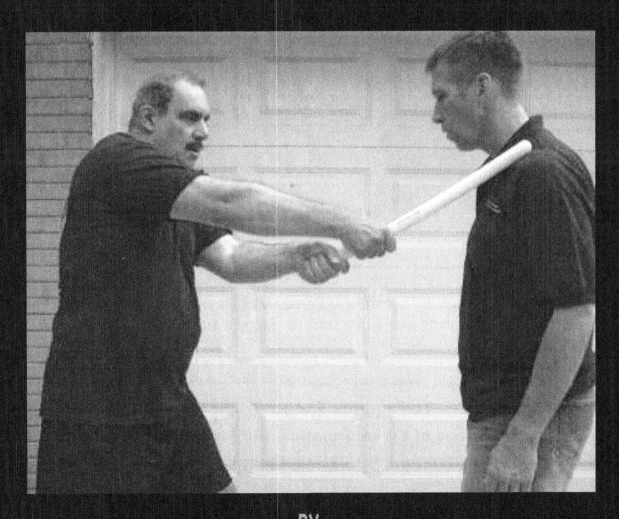

BY
JOSEPH J. TRUNCALE AND FERNAN VARGAS

THE PRO-SYSTEMS COMPLETE STRAIGHT BATON MANUAL

FOR POLICE & SECURITY OFFICERS

BY

JOSEPH J. TRUNCALE AND FERNAN VARGAS

SPECIAL NOTICE: The authors and publisher take no responsibility for the use or misuse of the information and techniques in this text. This book was written for informational purposes only.

TABLE OF CONTENTS

INTRODUCTION: The goal and purpose of this manual.........................4

Chapter One: Basic Nomenclature, Terms and Patterns of Movement:.........5

Chapter Two: Vulnerable areas of the body, baton grips, carries:.................7

Chapter Three: Baton Retention Techniques:...10

Chapter Four: Basic Baton Draws &One-hand long grip blocking techniques:.15

Chapter Five: Two-hand basic grip blocking techniques:..........................21

Chapter Six: Reverse grip blocking techniques:...................................22

Chapter Seven: One-hand long grip striking techniques:..........................23

Chapter Eight: Two-hand long grip striking techniques:...........................25

Chapter Nine: Reverse Grip striking techniques:...................................28

Chapter Ten: Sword Grip Striking techniques:......................................31

Chapter Eleven: Control and takedown techniques using the straight baton:....33

Chapter Twelve: Using the straight baton for self-defense situations:.............39

Chapter Thirteen: How to defend against a club or baton attack:...................49

Chapter Fourteen: Lethal Force Techniques 52

Chapter Fourteen: Ground Applications 60

Chapter Sixteen: Training Drills..67

Chapter Fourteen: The Warrior Philosophy and winning mind-set:.................71

Conclusion:..73

References and Resources:..74

About the authors:...75

Other books and manuals by the authors:................................78

SPECIAL THANKS:...81

INTRODUCTION

THE GOAL AND PURPOSE OF THIS MANUAL

The original Straight Baton course I had wrote for my agency (Glenview P.D.) has long been out of print, but I also wrote the original Monadnock: Use of the Straight Baton Book, which the MEB (Monadnock Expandable Baton) course is based upon; nevertheless, I had a request write my complete Pro-Systems and Bushi Satori Ryu straight baton program. This text will serve as the official guide to THE PRO-SYSTEMS COMPLETE STRAIGHT BATON COURSE MANUAL.

The goal and purpose is to provide a historical record of these techniques and a basic guide to straight baton training for law enforcement, security and for anyone interested in self-defense using the 24 to 36 inch batons. It is true that recent studies have shown that most police officers today rely on pepper spray, electronic devises, and empty hands to control resisting subjects. It seems recent research indicates that using the baton to defend against attackers and controlling resisting subjects is no longer popular with most police officers today.

I guess I am just an old fashioned retired police officer, but I personally think the police baton will always have a place in law enforcement for self-defense and control. It is hoped this straight baton book can be used as a reference source and guide for those interested in how to use the straight baton for control and self-defense.

The straight stick has probably been used as a self-defense tool since a human made the first footprints on earth. Through the ages variations of the stick and staff have been created to make a better self-defense tool. The straight stick was turned into spears and swords. Understanding the basic use of the straight police baton makes it possible to use numerous other objects for self-defense. In fact, the same techniques taught for using the police baton relate to a host of stick fighting and sword arts such as Hanbo-Jutsu, Jo-Jutsu, Wakizashi-Jutsu and similar weapon combat systems.

It is hoped this book will provide a basic overview of the many ways a straight baton can be used for self-defense, control and takedowns for law enforcement, security officers and martial artists studying weapons.

CHAPTER ONE

BATON NOMENCLATURE, TERMS AND PATTERNS OF MOVEMENT

The basic nomenclature of all straight batons, whether the expandable or solid one piece batons are similar. The standard rigid straight baton can be made of wood, metal or plastic. The standard size of baton officers and security officers carry is from 24 to 26 inches in length, but riot batons are 36 inches in length. The expandable baton models will be easier to carry because when closed they are about 8 inches in length. There are also two basic types of expandable batons. (1) Friction lock batons are made of three round metal pieces which will lock out by centrifugal force, using your arm to force it open. ((2) The positive lock batons are also made of three round metal pieces but can be locked open by just pulling it with your hands or using centrifugal force. The advantage of the positive lock batons is that they will not collapse when using them which the friction lock can sometimes do.

Standard Nomenclature of straight batons: There are four parts of the straight baton.

(1) The Grip portion is the part of the baton you would grasp with your hand.

(2) The Grip end is the portion of the baton at the end of the grip portion.

(3) The Long Portion is the main part of the baton.

(4) The Long End is the opposite area of the grip end.

KEY TERMS:

(1) Strong Hand is your dominant hand.

(2) Strong Foot is your dominant foot.

(3) Strong Side is any movement or technique done on your strong hand side.

(4) Support Hand is your least dominant hand.

(5) Support Foot is your least dominant foot.

(6) Support Side is any movement or technique done on your support hand side.

Stance and patterns of movement:

It is essential to understand the importance of good balance and body movement in any psychomotor skill class whether it is unarmed tactics or the use of the baton.

Basic Stance: Your legs should slightly bent and be shoulder width apart with your support side leg forward. Either both hands should be at chest level or your lead (support side) hand should be at chest level with the baton in your strong side hand.

Patterns of Movement: It is important to stay in a balanced position when moving. Begin practicing each movement from the basic stance position.

Forward Shuffle: Slide your lead (Support Side) foot about 12 inches forward followed by your rear (Strong side) foot.

Rear Shuffle: Slide your rear (Strong Side) foot about 12 inches backward followed by your front (Support Side) foot.

Strong Side Step: Slide your rear (Strong Side) foot to the side about 12 inches followed by your front (Support Side) foot.

Support Side Step: Slide your front (Support Side) foot to the side about 12 inches followed by your rear (Strong Side) foot.

Full Step Forward: Begin by pushing off on your rear (Strong) foot taking a full step so that now your rear foot becomes your lead foot.

Full Step Backward: Begin by pushing backward with your lead (Support) foot taking a full step so that your front foot now becomes your rear foot.

CHAPTER TWO

VULNERABLE AREAS OF THE BODY, BATON GRIPS, AND CARRIES

Police and security officers must be aware of the use of force policy of their agency when it comes to using the straight baton. This section provides a basic outline which can be used as a guide but each individual agency may have different policies when it comes to using the baton to strike a resisting subject. The following vulnerable areas are used by many law enforcement and security agencies teaching the use of the straight baton. The **TRAUMA RISK** of striking these areas is the basis of using the three color codes of **GREEN AREAS, YELLOW AREAS AND RED AREAS.** They can serve the same basic guideline as the traffic lights do when you drive.

TERMS:

Green Areas: These are parts of the human body which are less likely to cause any serious and lasting injury. They are considered primary target zones. They include the hands, inside of wrist, forearm, upper arm, shoulder area, thighs, calf, instep, shin, feet, rib cage (but not the solar Plexus), and lower abdomen areas.

Yellow Areas: These are parts of the body when struck that may cause a higher risk for significant injury to a subject. Depending on the TOTALITY OF THE SITUATION, you may decide a strike to this secondary target area is needed to stop a subject's aggressive action. These are considered secondary zones. Collarbone, elbow joint, groin, knee joint, chest area.

Red Areas: These are considered high risk areas and should be avoided unless you are in danger of "great bodily harm or of being killed" by your assailant. In this case, you must be aware of the law and liability factors in your jurisdiction. These high risk target areas include: Kidneys, neck, throat, solar plexus, spine and tail bone, ears, eyes, hollow behind ears and temple.

STRAIGHT BATON GRIPS, CARRIES

There are five methods to grip the straight baton in the Pro-Systems course. They include the one-hand basic grip, the two-hand long grip, the one-hand reverse grip, the two-hand reverse grip, which can be with either using an open or closed hand, and the sword grip.

STRAIGHT BATON GRIPS:

One-hand basic grip

Two-hand long grip

One-hand reverse grip

Two-hand reverse grip

Two-hand sword grip

STRAIGHT BATON CARRIES:

You can carry your baton in a holder on your support side or your strong side if it does not interfere with drawing your service weapon out. Other ways to carry your baton include: One-hand vertical carry, One-hand outside the arm carry, Two-hand long grip carry, One-hand and Two-hand reverse grip carry.

One-hand vertical carry   One-hand outside of arm carry

Two-hand long grip carry   One-hand and Two-hand reverse grip carry

CHAPTER THREE

STRAIGHT BATON RETENTION TECHNIQUES

There will be times in the line of duty that an officer may face a subject who is attempting to disarm the officer and secure their baton. Presented below are several strategies and techniques that an officer can utilize to secure their baton while in a conflict situation. All techniques should be used only when deemed appropriate by the officer based on the existing threat level. There will be times when the officer feels it is safer to retain the baton, and others when it is safer to sacrifice the baton in favor of another force option, such as a firearm.

The Officer must remember that a subject attempting to gain their baton immediately creates the possibility of a lethal force situation. Officers are trained in the proper use of the baton and in their hands it can effectively be utilized as a less lethal force option tool.

A subject armed with an officers baton however is unlikely to be trained in proper baton methods and is likely to use the baton in a manner which would constitute lethal force. In close proximity, with means and opportunity the attempt to disarm an officer is a clear sign of intent to harm. With means, opportunity, and intent present a dangerous scenario is created for the officer.

It is important to understand how to maintain control of your baton if it is grabbed by an assailant. The following technique is based upon the half circle principle. A subject grasps your baton with two hands attempting to grab it from you. (1) Lower your center of gravity by bending your legs. (2) At the same time grasp the long end portion of the baton. (3) Rotate the baton quickly in a half circle pushing downward breaking the assailant's grip. Move into a defensive position to counter any other move by the assailant. You may have to strike the subject to stop further attacks on your baton.

ATTACKER GRABS THE BATON WITH TWO HANDS: While carrying the baton in the reverse grip the attacker grabs the grip portion with both hands. The defender grasps the grip end portion and rotates the baton in a half circle, breaking the grip on his baton. He follows up with a reverse grip front strike.

1

2

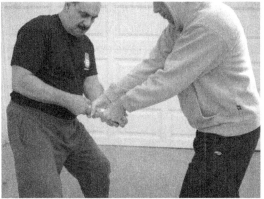

3

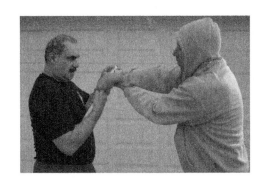

4

5

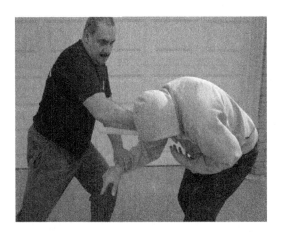

ATTACKER GRABS THE BATON FROM THE REAR WITH TWO HANDS: The defender pulls the baton forward with both hands and then using the momentum of the attacker pulling on the baton, drives the long end back into the attacker's chest.

1 2 3

ATTACKER GRABS THE BATON ON THE SIDE USING BOTH HANDS: The defender reaches under and grabs the opposite end of the baton and rotates the baton to a vertical position. The defender then drives the end of the baton downward breaking the hold. Defensive strikes can also be done to insure the attacker does not attempt another baton grab.

1 2

3 4

TWO HANDED WRIST GRAB

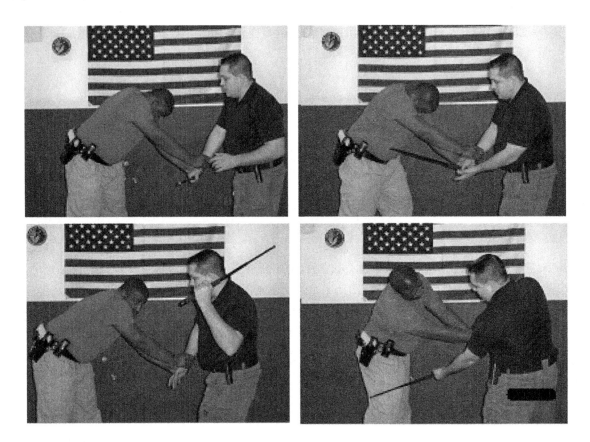

1.-2. The subject grabs the officers wrist with two hands.

2-3. The officer quickly passes the baton to his free hand

4. The officer executes a stunning blow to the subjects thigh, effecting a release.

IMPACT RETENTION

If an officer finds themselves struggling to retain their baton, and deem that it is necessary to retain the baton, the officer should use every tool available to them to maintain their weapon. Officers can use stunning blows such as hand, elbow, knee and foot strikes to diminish the subject and retain the baton.

CHAPTER FOUR

BASIC BATON DRAWS AND ONE-HAND LONG GRIP BLOCKS

The following are the basic baton drawing techniques and blocking techniques. The drawing techniques include the cross draw, the two-hand thrust draw and the rear draw. NOTE: If you carry an expandable straight baton you should also practice expanding the baton open as you draw your baton.

DRAWING THE BATON

Arguably the most important aspect of baton training is training the draw. A force option tool is of no use to you if you can not bring it into play effectively when you require it. Presented here are three baton draws which give the officers the option of wearing the baton on the strong side or the support side.

STRONG SIDE DRAW

When drawing from the strong side the officer should reach down with the strong hand and grip the baton firmly. Once the baton has been gripped the officer should pull the baton upwards removing it from the holster. The officer is now in a good position to transition to a conflict stance or to an opening technique.

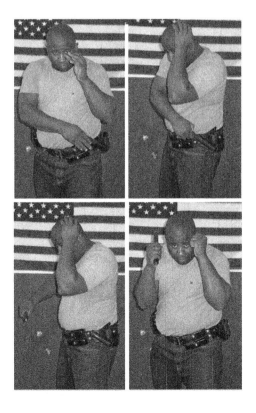

CROSS DRAW

The officer begins to reach across his body with his rear hand to the baton on their support side. The officer raises their support side arm vertically in front of their body as they reach for the baton to shield themselves from attack while drawing the baton. The officer continues to draw the baton while the support arm shields the officer. Once the baton is drawn the officer should assume a conflict stance

SUPPORT SIDE DRAW AND HAND SWITCH

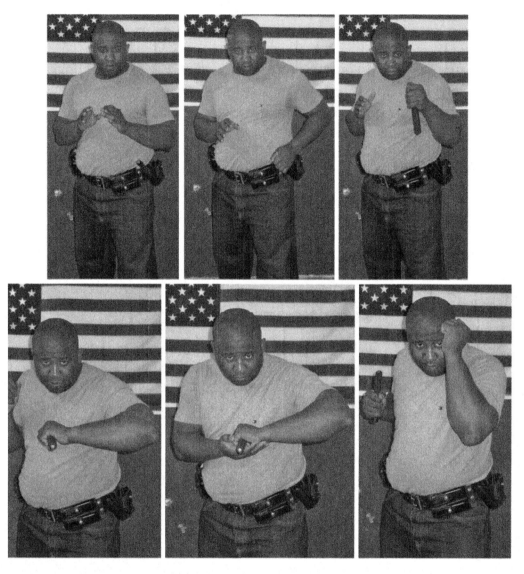

Officers who carry a firearm on their strong side will usually opt to carry a baton on their support side. If the baton is carried tip down on the support side the officer can safely draw the baton with the support hand in the following manner. The officer will begin from the traditional interview stance. The officer then brings their support hand to the baton. The officer draws the baton upwards in front of their body (note the officer can use closed baton tactics at this point.) The officer will then tilt the baton horizontally at their centerline. The tip of the baton should be facing the subject. The officer then passes baton from the support hand into the rear hand (the baton is not

in the rear hand tip up position) The officer then adopts a conflict stance. Note that the baton is now tip up and ready to be opened.

OPENING THE BATON

When opening the baton, the officer should be sure to do so when there is a window of safety. Attempting to open the baton during a physical conflict may not be the most secure option for an officer. If the officer feels that they can not safely open the baton, they should use Defensive tactics and movement to create a window of opportunity. Other wise the officer should use closed baton tactics until the opportunity arises for safe opening of the baton.

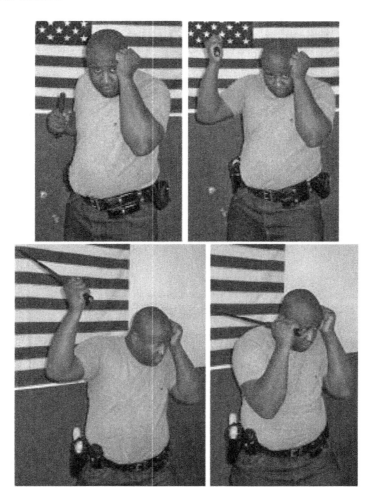

ONE BATON OPEN TO THE SKY

From a conflict stance the officer should pull their hand back diagonally over their strong side shoulder (the motion is similar to pulling the cord on a lawn mower). The arm should extend far out and once it reaches full extension the officer should jerk back. This motion will ensure a good secure opening of the baton. Once the officer opens the baton they should return to a conflict stance.

BATON OPEN TO THE GROUND

From a conflict stance the officer should forcefully swing the baton downward towards the ground on the side of their strong side leg. Once the baton opens the officer should continue to circle the arm upwards and back to a conflict stance.

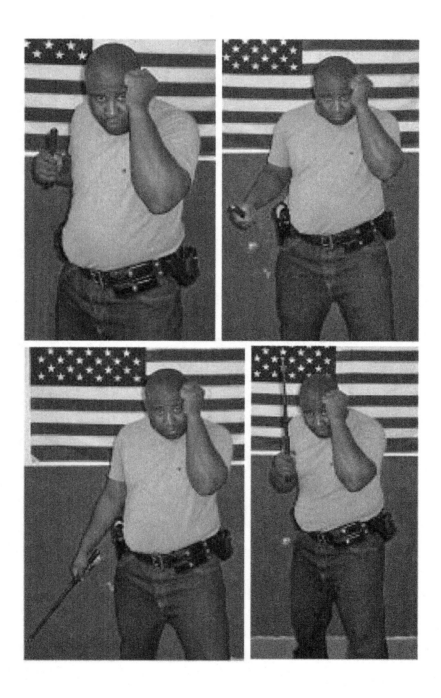

Baton Cross Draw: With your support hand grasp the long portion and push it forward while at the same time grasp the grip portion with your strong hand drawing out the baton. You can either place your baton downward or on the side of the shoulder

Two-hand draw: Grasp the baton while it is in the ring or holder with both hands and drive the baton forward. **Rear Draw:** Slide the baton to the rear with your support hand while at the same time grasping the grip portion with your right hand drawing the baton to the rear.

Basic One Hand Blocks:

High Block

Low Block

Strong Side Block   Support Side Block

CHAPTER FIVE

TWO-HAND LONG GRIP BLOCKS

The Pro-Systems Straight Baton course has five basic long grip blocks. They are Strong Side Block, Support Side Block, High Block, Middle Block and Low Block.

Strong Side block   Support Side block   High block

Middle block   Low block

CHAPTER SIX

REVERSE GRIP BLOCKING TECHNIQUES

The Pro-Systems Straight Baton course has five basic two-hand reverse grip blocks. They are High Block, Low Block, Strong Side Block, Support Side Block and Middle Block.

TWO-HAND REVERSE GRIP BLOCKS:

1   High Block   2   Low Block

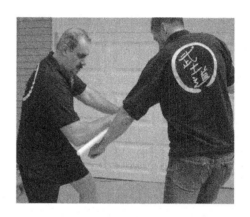

3   Left Side (Inside) Block   4   Right Side (Outside) Block

Middle Block

CHAPTER SEVEN

ONE-HAND LONG GRIP STRIKING TECHNIQUES

There are four basic one-hand long grip striking angles in this course. They are the upward strike, downward strike, forward strike and reverse strike. It is important to strike all the way through the target when striking training bags. ALWAYS STRIKE THROUGH THE TARGET AND DO NOT BOUNCE BACK BECAUSE IT REDUCES THE POWER OF THE STRIKING TECHNIQUES. THIS IS THE KEY TO POWERFUL STRIKES.

One-Hand Long Grip Strikes:

Upward Strike   Downward strike

Forward Strike: Follow all the way through with this strike.

Reverse Strike: Begin this strike when you have completed the forward strike and the baton is on your support side.

TRAINING BAG PRACTICE: You should always practice the straight baton striking techniques using training bags to develop power and accuracy. Below shows practicing the forward and reverse strikes using the one-hand grip method.

CHAPTER EIGHT

TWO-HAND LONG GRIP STRIKES

There are numerous two-hand long grip strikes in the Pro-Systems Baton Course. They include the front jab/thrust, rear jab/thrust, left side jab/thrust, right side jab/thrust, left middle hook, right middle hook, left low hook, right low hook and middle strike (Same as Middle block technique).

Two-Hand Long Position Grip Jabs/Thrusts: The only difference between a

Jab and a Thrust is a jab is a quick forward and back movement and a thrust is a strike that goes through the target deeper. It is the difference between a boxers left jab and left hook punches. The jab distracts and the hook knocks out.

Front Jab/thrust   Rear Jab/thrust

   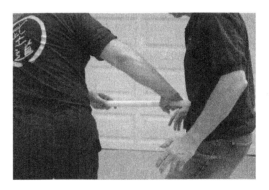

Left Side Jab/ Thrust   Right Side Jab/Thrust

Two-Hand Left & Right Hook Strikes:

1   Left Side Hook Middle Strike

2   Right Side Hook Middle Strike

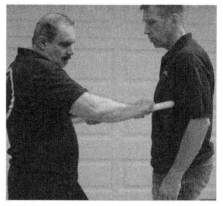

3   Left Side Low Hook Strike

4   Right Side Low Hook Strike

BAG PRACTICE USING THE TWO-HAND LONG GRIP:

Front Jab/ Thrust practice on the training bag.

Rear Jab/Thrust and left and right hook strikes on the training bag.

CHAPTER NINE

REVERSE GRIP STRIKING TECHNIQUES

There are many basic reverse grip striking techniques in the Pro-Systems complete straight baton course. They are the one-hand front jab, one-hand rear jab, left side one-hand jab, right side one-hand jab, two-hand forward thrust, two-hand rear thrust, two-hand forward swing strike, two-hand reverse swing strike, two-hand left side thrust, two-hand right side thrust, two-hand downward swing strike and two-hand upward swing strike.

Reverse Grip One-Hand Jabs

| 1 | Front Jab | 2 | Rear Jab |

| 3 | Left Side Jab | 4 | Right Side Jab |

Reverse Grip Two-Hand Thrusts:

1   Front Thrust   2   Rear Thrust   3

4   Left Side Thrust   5   Right Side Thrust

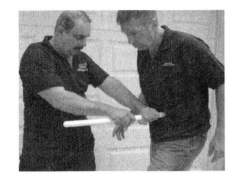 

Reverse Grip Swing Strikes:

1   **Upward Swing Strike**   2

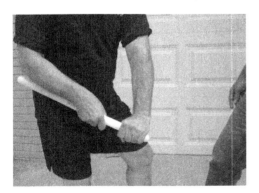 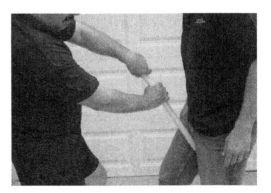

3   **Downward Swing Strike**   4

5   **Forward Swing Strike**   6

7   **Reverse Swing Strike**   8

CHAPTER TEN

SWORD GRIP STRIKING TECHNIQUES

One of the primary differences between the majority of straight baton programs and the Pro-Systems course is that we include two-hand sword grip strikes. The reason is simple; the sword grip strikes are the most powerful of all the striking techniques. If you are dealing with a person on drugs or is intoxicated you may have to use the sword grip to stop the subject from resisting arrest. Further, using the two-hand sword grip can be effective against someone with a weapon such as a club, tie iron or knife.

The following sword striking techniques are in the Pro-Systems complete straight baton program. Upward strike, downward strike, forward cross body strike, reverse cross body strike, forward straight thrust strike. Note: The overhead position and the side of your head are two Sword Positions called Jodan (High guard position) and Hasso (Side of head position)

Two-Hand Sword Strikes:

1   Upward Strike into Groin   2

3   Downward Strike to Shoulders   4

5 Forward Cross Body Strike to Thigh   6

7   Reverse Cross Body Strike   8

Straight thrust using the sword grip.

CHAPTER ELEVEN

CONTROL AND TAKEDOWN TECHNIQUES USING THE BATON

Police and security officers need to know how to use the straight baton to control a resisting subject and to take down a resisting subject for handcuffing. These are just a few of the many control and takedown techniques we teach in the Pro-Systems and Bushi Satori Ryu courses. Keep in mind that these techniques can be very painful and you should always practice slowly until you master the technique; however, you should also practice with speed and control once you master a particular technique.

Long Position Grip Locks and Takedowns: Arm Locks & Arm Bars

Strong Side Arm Lock: (1) Place long portion between upper arm and body and grab the end portion with your left hand. (2) Rotate baton into a rear arm-lock. (3-4) Finish hold by placing your hand on the subject's shoulder.

1

2

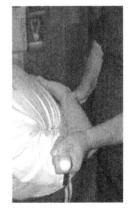

3

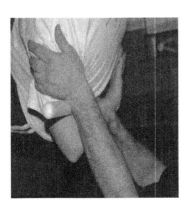

4

Note: A variation is to wrap your arm around the baton and place the subject in a rear arm lock and you can also remove the baton.

You can also take the subject to the ground using the arm lock takedown in order to handcuff the subject. IMPORTANT NOTE: In order to practice the arm lock on the subject's opposite arm you must use the baton in your support side arm to perform the technique.

NOTE: YOU SHOULD PRACTICE THIS ARM LOCK USING BOTH YOUR RIGHT AND LEFT HANDS TO FULLY MASTER THIS TECHNIQUE.

<u>Arm-Bar Takedown:</u> Using the one-hand grip, grab the subject's wrist with your non-baton holding hand and pull subject's arm straight. Place the portion of the baton nearest to your hand on the back of the subject's elbow area. Push down on the subject's elbow as you pull upon the subject's wrist. **Note: The same ground lock up method is used on ALL TAKEDOWN AND LOCK UPS.**

1   2   3

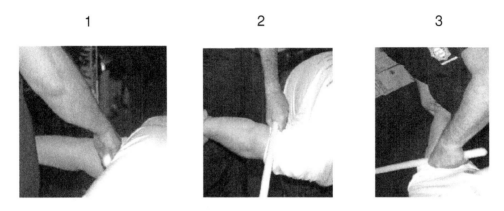

Reverse Grip Arm Locks and Takedowns: Place the grip portion just above the elbow while grasping the grip portion with your support side hand. Pull down as your apply the reverse grip arm-lock to the subject.

Strong Side Arm-Lock

1   2   3   4

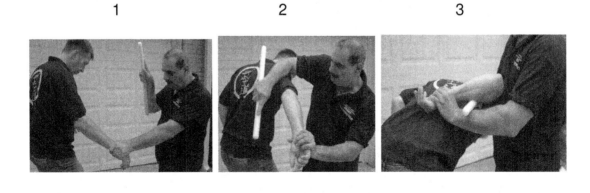

Support Side Arm-Lock (CLAMP): Grasp the subject's wrist with your support wide arm and move the baton over the subject's arm to complete the arm-lock.

1   2   3

Front X Lock Takedown: The subject attempts to grab your shirt or choke you. Using the reverse grip on your baton, rotate over the subject's forearm and grasp the opposite end of the baton drive downward completing the lock.

1   2

3   4

Rear X Lock Takedown: Using the reverse grip rotate the baton around the subject's wrist. Grasp the other end of the baton and rotate the baton downward.

1   2   3

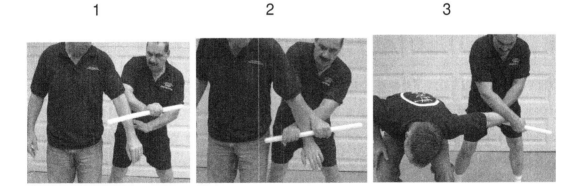

Reverse Grip Arm-Bar Takedown: Grasp the subject's wrist with your support hand as you place the baton just above the subject's elbow. Apply pressure downward moving into a ground lock up position.

1

2

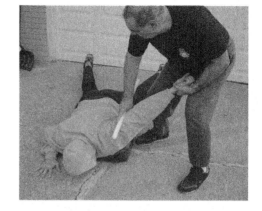

3

4

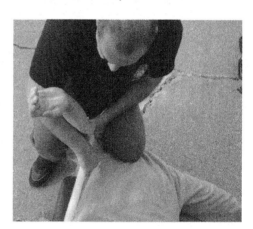

IMPORTANT NOTE: The ground lock ups are the same ones as shown in volume one of Pro-Systems Combatives. The ground lock-up is complete when you place one knee on the upper shoulder area and the other knee either on the ground next to the subject's upper shoulder area or up as shown in this photograph. The only difference is that a weapon (short stick, straight stick, side-handle baton) is used for the takedown.

CHAPTER TWELVE

USING THE STRAIGHT BATON FOR SELF-DEFENSE SITUATIONS

Sticks and stones were probably the first weapons used when humans began walking the earth. No doubt the first stick fighting methods were also developed early in the evolution of humankind. In more recent times the 26th president of the United States, Theodore Roosevelt was famous for the saying "Speak slowly and carry a bit stick."

This chapter will cover a few of the basic ways you can use the straight baton in a self-defense situations. You should also be aware of the use of force laws in your area if you decide to carry a baton or other type of straight stick for self-defense. Most of these techniques were taken from my Cane, and Hanbo-Jutsu self-defense manuals. IMPORTANT NOTE: These are just a few examples of using the baton for self-defense. Several book length books could be written on this self-defense topic alone.

FRONT TWO-HAND CHOKE DEFENSE #1: Attacker lunges at your throat using two-hands. Thrust the stick upward breaking the choke and follow up with a forward strike.

1	2	3

FRONT TWO-HAND CHOKE DEFENSE #2.

Using the two-hand sword grip drive stick

the stick upward into the attacker's groin.

REAR HAND CHOKE DEFENSE

Drive the stick upward to the rear

into the attacker's groin area.

TWO-ARM REAR CHOKE DEFENSE: As soon as the attacker places his arm around your neck, immediately release one hand and pull the attacker's arm down as you turn your head into the crook of the attacker's arm. Follow up with driving the stick upward into the attacker's groin.

1

2

FRONT UNDER THE ARMS BEAR HUG DEFENSE: A subject has you in a front bear hug. Place the baton/stick on the subject's head and neck area and drive downward breaking the hold. You may want to follow up with some striking techniques to insure no further attacks will follow.

3

4

FRONT OVER THE ARMS
BEAR HUG DEFENSE:

As the attacker grabs you drive the baton/stick upward into the attacker's groin.

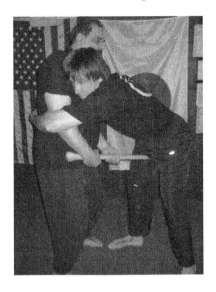

REAR AROUND THE ARMS
BEAR HUG DEFENSE:

As the attacker's arms grab you drive the baton to the rear upward into the attacker's groin.

FRONT CHARGING DEFENSE:

Using a two-hand grip thrust tip into throat.

FRONT KICK ATTACK COUNTER:

Using sword grip swing baton into groin.

ROUND KICK, LEFT AND RIGHT PUNCH COUNTER: Using the two-hand grip block the right round kick, slip the attacker's right punch and strike his ribs with the baton/stick and finish with strike to the attacker's jaw and neck area.

1

2

3

RIGHT ROUND HOUSE PUNCH COUNTER: Using the sword grip strike the attacker's right arm and counter with a strike at the attacker head or neck.

1

2

LEFT STRAIGHT PUNCH COUNTER: Using the sword grip strike the attacker's left arm and follow up with a counter strike at the attacker's neck and head area.

1   2

ARM GRAB ATTEMPT WHILE HOLDING THE BATON: Subject attempts a two-hand wrist grab while you are holding your baton. Drop your center of gravity as you use the half circle movement with your baton breaking the hold. If needed follow up with other strikes if the attacker continues to assault you.

1   2

WEAPON RETENTION USING THE STRAIGHT BATON: A subject makes an attempt to grab your service weapon while you are holding the baton in the reverse grip. Immediately apply downward pressure against the subject's hand and your gun, forcing the attacker's hands open and breaking the hold. Follow up with a baton strike to stop any further attacks on your service weapon. Note: This same technique and principle works while holding the baton in the two-hand long grip and one-hand grip on the baton.

1

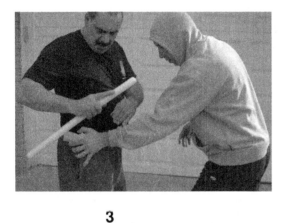

2

3

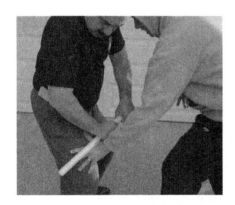

4

5

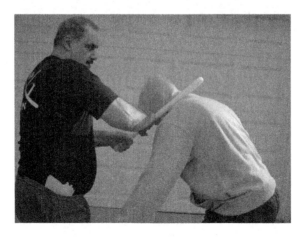

ONE-HAND GRAB DEFENSE: While holding the baton in the reverse grip an attacker grabs the wrist of your left hand. Immediately thrust the grip end tip into the stomach area of your attacker.

1 2

ONE-HAND CROSS GRAB DEFENSE: While holding the baton in the reverse grip an attacker grabs your left wrist with his right hand cross grab. Immediately rotate your left hand grasping the attacker's wrist while at the same time thrusting into the rib area of your attacker. You can also follow up with other strikes if needed.

1 2

3

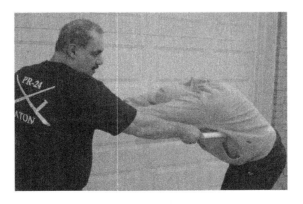

RIGHT WRIST GRAB WITH A RIGHT PUNCH DEFENSE: Attacker grabs your wrist and throws a right punch at the same time. Defender uses a left hand block while rotating the baton in a vertical position. Defender grasps the end of the baton and drives the baton downward breaking the attacker's grip. Follow up with strikes if needed.

1

2

3

 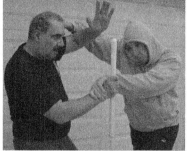 

4

5

6

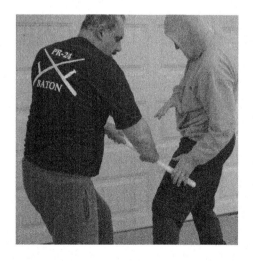

RIGHT PUNCH DEFENSE: Attacker throws a right punch. Defender using the reverse grip blocks the punch with his left hand and thrusts the grip end into the attacker's stomach area and finishes with an arm-lock takedown.

1

2

3

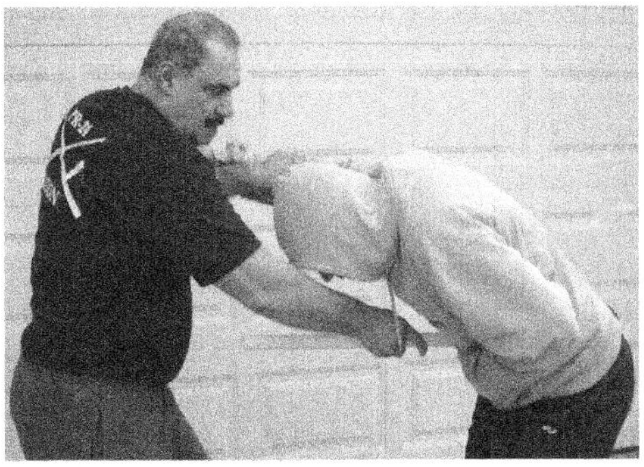

4

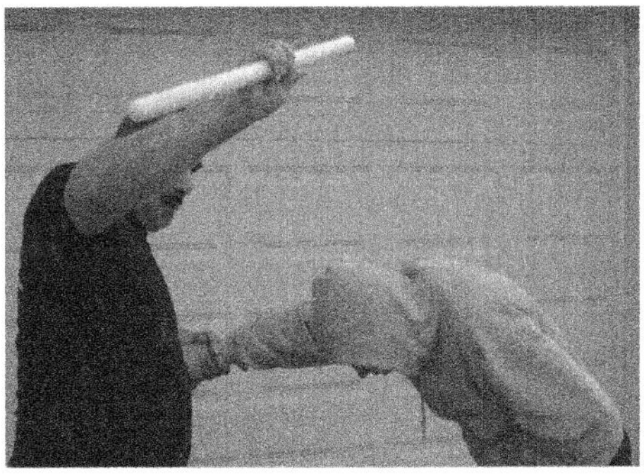

5

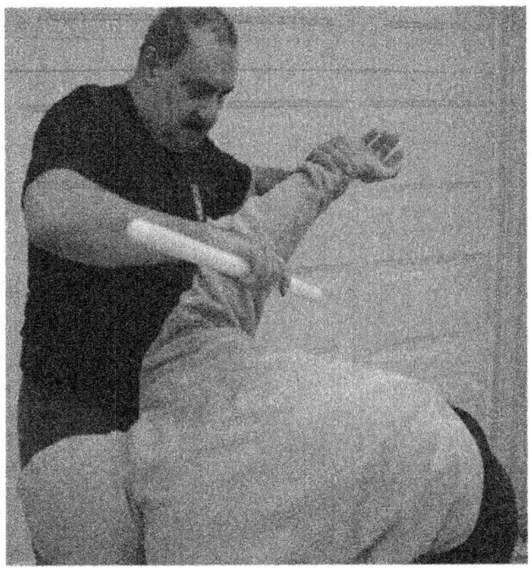

6

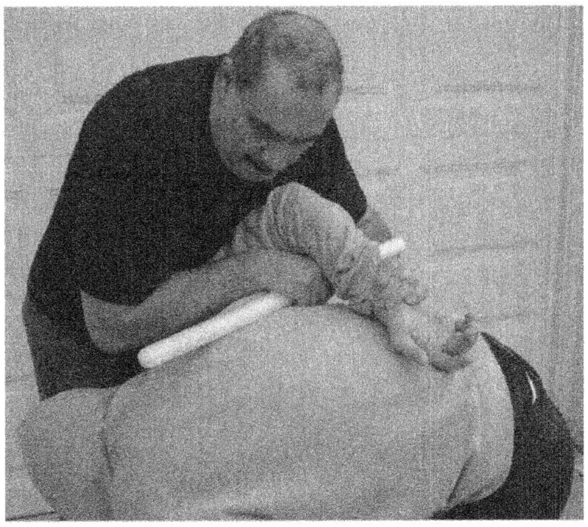

ATTACKER THROWS A RIGHT PUNCH: Holding the baton in the reverse grip an attacker throws a right punch at your face. The defender uses an inside open hand block and grasps the attacker's wrist while at the same time thrusting the end tip into the attacker's ribs. He follows up with an arm bar takedown.

1

2

3

4

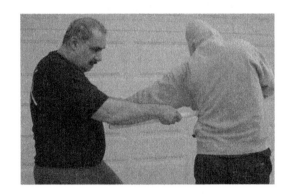

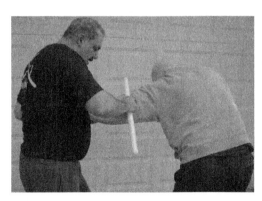

KNIFE ATTACK DEFENSE: Attacker attempts a forward slash with a knife. The defender blocks and grabs the attacker's wrist and at the same time drives the tip of the grip end into the attacker's throat. Note: There are numerous other self-defense techniques using the baton but it would take several volumes. These are just examples.

48

CHAPTER THIRTEEN

DEFENSES AGAINST A CLUB ATTACK

I have always loved weapons of all kinds and sought out anyone who could teach me how to use another weapon; however, I have also followed the philosophy that learning how to use a weapon must also include how to defend against that specific weapon as well. In this case, my straight baton course would not be complete without this chapter. The fact is, an attacker may successfully take away an officer's baton or the officer may find him or herself in a situation where the assailant has a club like weapon. The techniques and tactics in this chapter are the same ones in my Combatives manuals.

A LOW FORWARD STRIKE COUNTER: The key to defeating a weapon like a stick is to get inside the impact area if possible. This means moving into the subject rather than backing up. In this situation the attacker swings the baton at the defender's lower body area. The defender steps forward inside the impact area and uses a low block to stop the strike.

1

2

3

A HIGH FORWARD STRIKE COUNTER: Attacker swings his stick at your head area. Defender steps forward with his hands up inside the attacker's arm. The defender follows up with a forearm strike to the neck and a knee kick to the groin. The defender grasps the baton and twists it downward disarming the attacker.

1

2

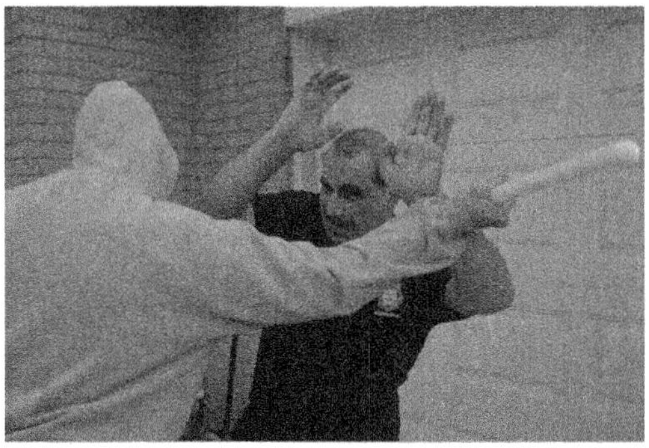

3

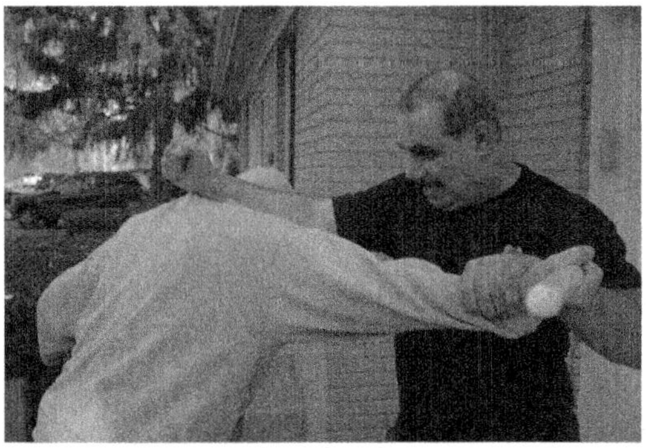

4

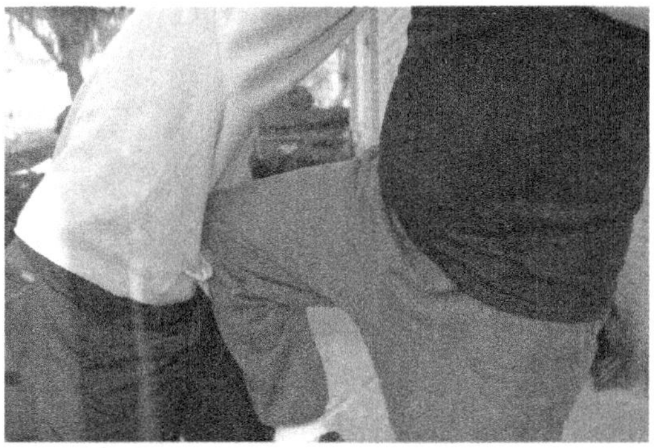

5

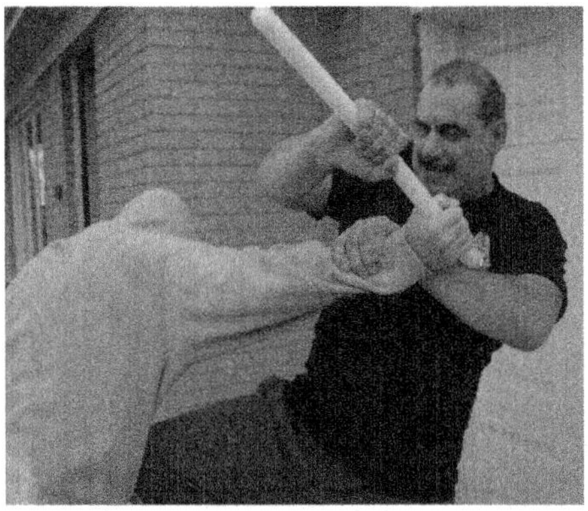

6

A TWO-HAND FORWARD THRUST COUNTER: The attacker attempts a two-hand forward thrust strike. The defender grabs the stick with his left hand and performs a right eye thrust and left front kick to the groin. The defender grabs the baton with both hands and twists it out of the attacker's hands and follows up with a strike to the attacker's shoulder area.

1

2

3

4

5

6

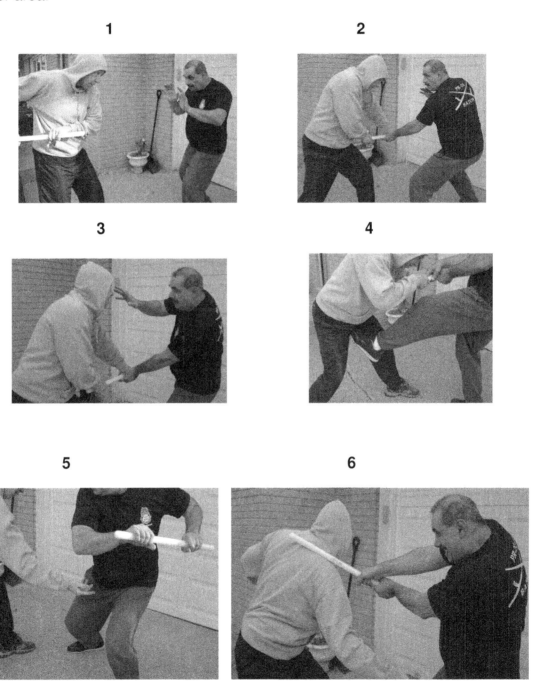

CHAPTER FOURTEEN

LETHAL FORCE COMBATIVES

There are times when an officer may need to use their baton as a lethal force tool in defense of their lives or the life of another. Should an officer find themselves at this threat level, they may use the following techniques.

NOTE, THE FOLLOWING TECHNIQUES ARE LIKELY TO CAUSE GREAT BODILY HARM OR DEATH. THE TECHNIQUES SHOULD NOT BE USED UNDER ANY CIRCUMSTANCES UNLESS

THE OFFICER STRONGLY BELIEVES THAT THEIR LIFE OR THE LIFE OF ANOTHER INDIVIDUAL IS IN DANGER AND ALL OTHER REASONABLE OPTIONS HAVE BEEN EXHUSTED.

The following techniques are appropriate to apply **<u>ONLY</u>** during a lethal force encounter.

- LF Striking
- Chokes
- Take Downs
- Ground Defense
- Weapon Retention

LETHAL FORCE STRIKING TECHNIQUES

Officers will rely on the striking techniques in their tool box as their primary lethal force options with the baton. Officers should carefully study the lethal force targets on the body in order to 1. Minimize damage and liability when not using lethal force, and 2. To be able to effectively target a lethal force target in a life or death situation.

LEVEL III: LETHAL FORCE STRIKING

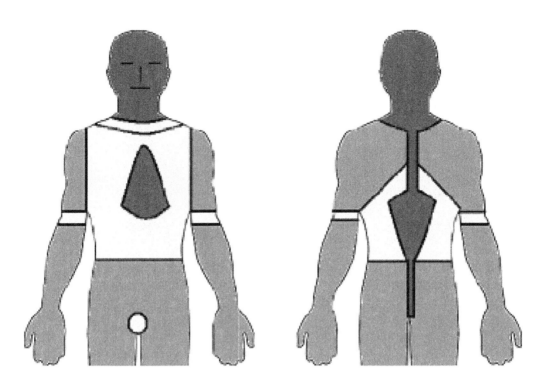

Level Three targets are last resort lethal force targets. An office should never attempt a stun to these targets unless the officer fears that the subject posses a threat of death or seriously injure to the officer or another.

Spine	Ear	Bridge of Nose	Eyes
Kidney	Throat	Lower Jaw	Tail Bone
Solar Plexus	Neck	Temple	Upper Jaw
Base of Neck	Groin		

UPWARD SMASH

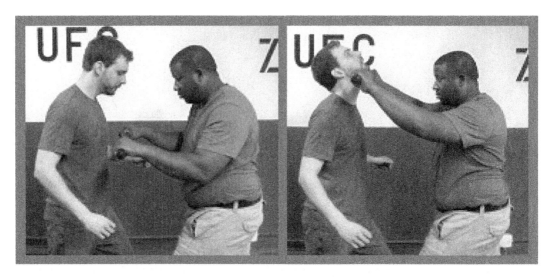

To execute the upward smash the officer assumes the two handed guard. The officer will hold the baton under the desired target and then rapidly lift upwards, moving at the elbow and shoulder to strike the target with the middle shaft of the baton.

DOWNWARD SMASH

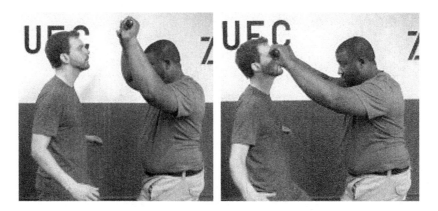

To execute the Downward smash the officer assumes the two handed guard. The officer will hold the baton above the desired target and then rapidly lift upwards, moving at the elbow and shoulder to strike the target with the middle shaft of the baton.

CHOKE HOLDS: FRONT CROSS CHOKE

The technique is applied by holding the baton in a reverse grip. The officer should place their wrist on the subject's neck on the same side. This will place the shaft of the baton across the back of the subject's neck. The officer should then cross his free hand and grip the baton shaft on the other side. The officer should have both wrists close to the subject's neck. Once secured the officer squeeze tight and pull his hands to his navel

.

REAR CROSS CHOKE

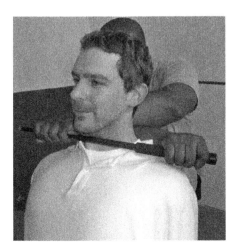

The technique is applied by holding the baton in a reverse grip. The officer should place their wrist on the subject's neck on the same side. This will place the shaft of the baton across the subject's throat. The officer should then cross his free hand and grip the baton shaft on the other side. The officer should have both wrists close to the subject's neck. Once secured the officer squeeze tight and pull his hands to his navel.

REAR CHOKE

To execute the rear choke, the officer must start by placing the baton across the subjects neck or throat. Once the baton is in place the officer will insert their free hand and place the end shaft of the baton in the pit of the elbow of the free hand. The officer next will place his free hand behind the subjects head at the base of the skull. The Officer now will simultaneously push the head down, while squeezing his elbows in tight to his own body and extending his lateral muscles

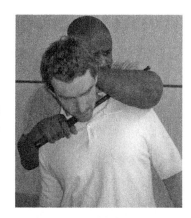

REAR PULLING CHOKE

To execute the rear pulling choke, the officer must first extend the baton across the subjects neck directly below their chin. The officers hands should be snug on both sides

of the subjects neck. The officer then secures the baton from both sides and pulls both hands to his own waist while stepping back to ensure the subject does not fall directly on him.

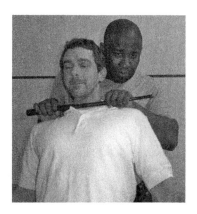

CHOKE HOLDS: DIAGONAL PULLING CHOKE

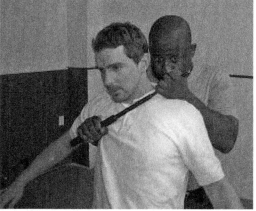

To execute the rear Diagonal pulling choke, the officer must first extend the baton under the subjects arm pit and across the chest. The officer will grip the baton on the opposite end. The officer then secures the baton from both sides and pulls both hands to his own waist while stepping back to ensure the subject does not fall directly on him.

TAKE DOWN: HIP PULL TAKE DOWN

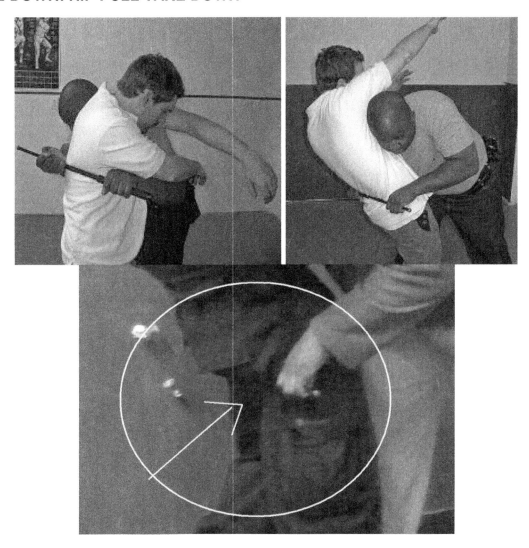

1. Begin by wrapping the baton around the assailants back.

2. Lower the baton around the assailants waist while simultaneously puling the baton

towards your own torso and pushing into the assailant with your shoulder. Make sure

your head is to the outside of the assailants body.

3. Once the assailant begins to loose balance, release one side of the baton to release the assailant so they fall to the ground without the officer going to the ground.

A safer variation of the take down which does not go against the spine is pictured in the third photograph. Here the officer wraps behind the subjects buttocks rather than the swell of the back. the take down is equally effective.

DOUBLE LEG TAKEDOWN

1. Begin by wrapping the baton around the assailants back.

2. Lower the baton around the assailants waist while simultaneously puling the baton towards your own torso and pushing into the assailant with your shoulder. Make sure your head is to the outside of the assailants body.

3. Once the assailant begins to loose balance, Drop the baton behind their knees and continue to drive with the shoulder. Release one side of the baton to release the assailant so they fall to the ground without the officer going to the ground.

HEAD PULL TAKE DOWN

To execute the head pull take down, the officer must first extend the baton across back of the subjects neck. The officers hands should be snug on both sides of the subjects neck. The officer then secures the baton from both sides and pulls both hands to his own waist while stepping back to ensure the subject does not fall directly on him.

CHAPTER FIFTEEN

GROUND APPLICATIONS

There are times when an officer may find themselves on the ground during an altercation. If the officer finds themselves in this position they should first seek to establish a good defensive position and then Safely make the transition back to the standing position. Officers should practice applying all of the standing baton techniques on the on the ground as well, as they translate effectively. Some considerations must be made as well as adjustments but the overall theories and strategies are still very sound. Bellow are a series of sequences which are meant to be a small skill set. The officer must add to this skill set through the use flexible application of the standing core techniques to ground situations. This will be best accomplished by the use of Functional training drill.

Officers should also note that Ground techniques are potentially lethal force scenarios for two reasons. 1. The officer is in a compromised position where they are not able to properly defend themselves and 2. because in order to apply some of the ground fighting techniques the officer must apply stress to the joints, and other areas such as the spine, or kidneys. Even though the officer is applying slow direct pressure and not impact force, the effected areas of the subjects body are sensitive and the officer can not ensure that the application of the technique will be 100% safe for the subject.

MOUNT DEFENSE #1

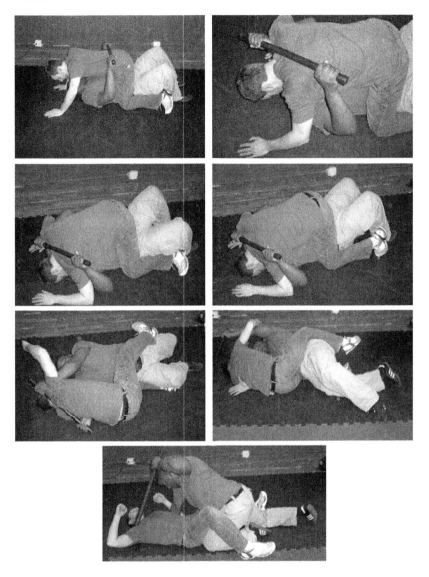

1. The officer finds himself mounted by the subject. The officer wraps the baton around the subjects back.

2. The officer brings the baton across the subjects shoulder

3. The officer pulls the subject into him towards the ground.

4. The officer now raises his hips, further putting the subject off balance.

5-6. The officer now rolls to towards the subjects trapped shoulder, rolling the subject off of the officer.

7. The officer then assumes a ready position, where he can strike or disengage.

SCISSOR SWEEP

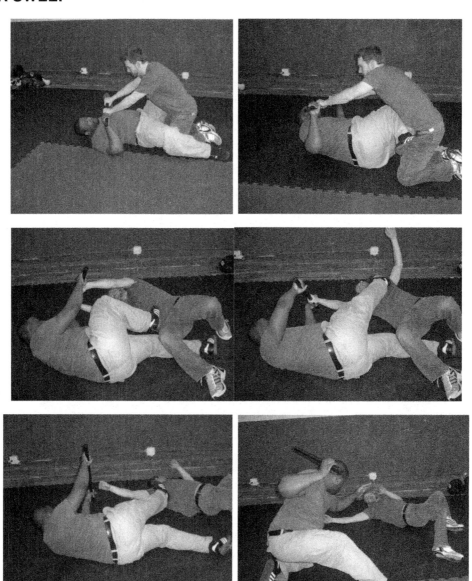

1. The officer finds the subject in his guard fighting for the officers baton. The subject has two hands on the baton

2. Turn to side, and then Scissor your legs, while pulling the secured arm.

3-4. Once the subject has been taken over, the officer kicks the subjects arm to free his grip on the baton.

5.The officer then kicks to the other arm to free the baton entirely.

6. The officer now assumes a defensive stance while returning to his feet.

MOUNT DEFENSE #2

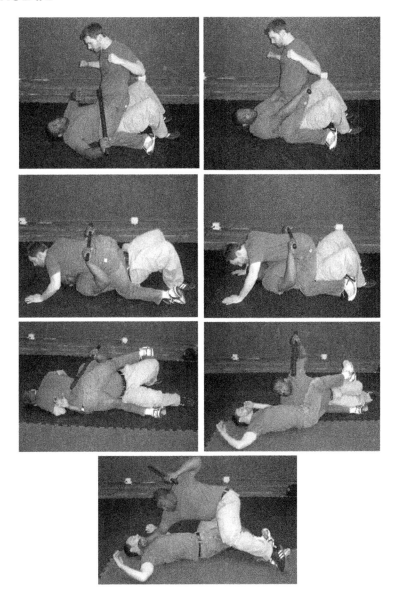

1. The officer finds himself mounted by the subject. The officer wraps the baton around

the subjects back.

2. The officer brings the baton across the subjects shoulder

3. The officer pulls the subject into him towards the ground.

4. The officer now raises his hips, further putting the subject off balance.

5-6. The officer now rolls to towards the subjects trapped shoulder, rolling the subject off of the officer.

7. The officer then assumes a ready position, where he can strike or disengage.

TWO HANDED ANKLE PICK:

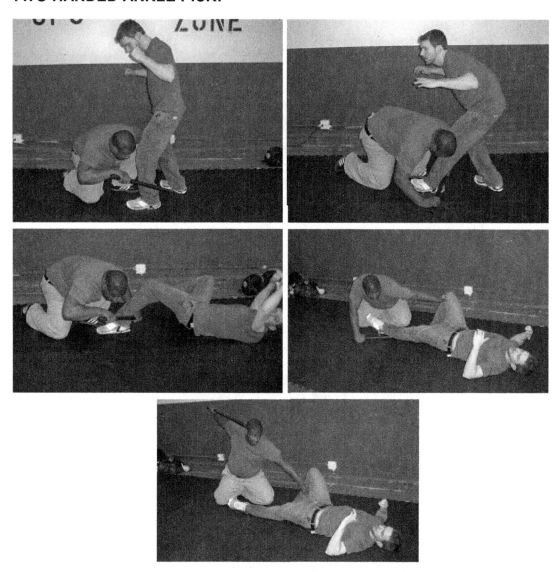

1. Officer takes his baton and places it behind the assailant's ankle.

2-3. The officer will use their shoulder to apply slow and direct pressure to the thigh or shin or knee. *Note the officer keeps his head to the outside of the subject's body.

4. The officer monitors the subject's legs to avoid being struck with a kick.

5. The officer is now ready to retreat to his feet.

DOUBLE LEG TAKE DOWN

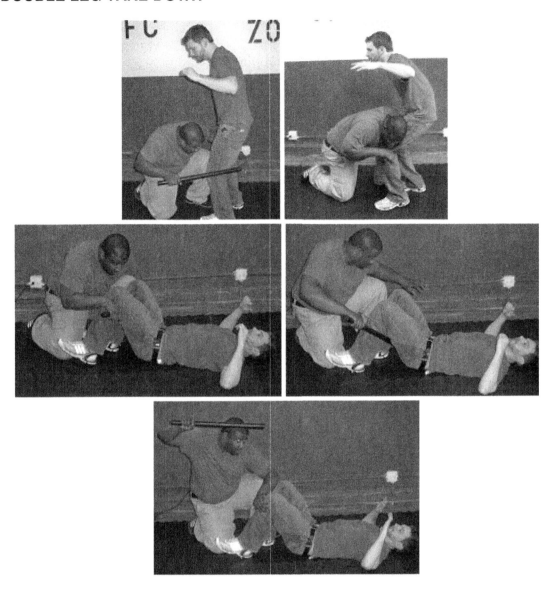

1. Officer takes his baton and places it behind the assailant's knees.

2. The officer will use their shoulder to apply slow and direct pressure to the thigh or shin

or knee. *Note the officer keeps his head to the outside of the subject's body.

3.-4. The officer releases one end of the baton in order to free it from behind the subjects legs.

5. The officer monitors the subject's legs to avoid being struck with a kick. And is now

ready to retreat to his feet.

GROUND STRIKING

All of the striking techniques in the Manual are equally applicable from the various ground positions. The Thrusting strikes presented below are for illustrative purposes.

CHAPTER SIXTEEN

FUNCTIONAL TRAINING DRILLS

OBSTRUCTED ATTACK SOLUTIONS

There will be times when the officer is attempting to complete and attack and the subject creates an obstruction to this attack. The officer has several ways to properly address the obstructed attack. They include:

-Pulling the obstructing limb

-Pushing the obstructed limb

-Taking a secondary line of attack

OBSTRUCTED ATTACK SOLUTION: THE PULL

1. The assailant blocks and obstructs the officers initial attack.

2. The Officer uses his free hand to pull the obstruction away

3. The officer is then free to counter attack if needed.

OBSTRUCTED ATTACK SOLUTION: THE PUSH

1. The assailant blocks and obstructs the officers initial attack.

2. The Officer uses his free hand to push the obstruction away

3. The officer is then free to counter attack if needed.

OBSTRUCTED ATTACK SOLUTION:SECONDARY LINES

1. The assailant blocks and obstructs the officers initial attack.

2. The Officer pulls his initial attack away from the obstruction and finds an unobstructed path on which to complete the attack.

3. The officer is then free to counter attack if needed.

MEET & FOLLOW THE FORCE

One excellent drill for developing hand-eye coordination, timing and reaction time is the Meet & Follow Force Drill. As the assailant Attacks the officer , the officer will meet the incoming attack with his weapon, coming to the inside of the opponents arc of power. Meeting the force is most often a proactive way of addressing an incoming attack.

FOLLOW THE FORCE DRILL SERIES

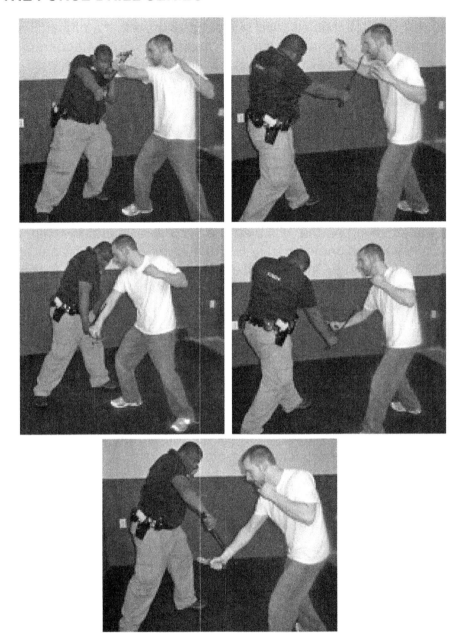

As the assailant Attacks the officer , the officer is not prepared and is not quick enough to meet the incoming attack with his weapon, coming to the inside of the opponents arc of power. The officer then uses body movement to avoid the attack and then address the attack on the "back end" by following the attack. Following the force is a most often a Reactive way of addressing an incoming attack.

Spontaneous Defense Drill

To perform this drill, multiple subjects will surround and circle the officer. The subject's will take turns randomly attacking the officer. The attacks will be staggered so the officer can not time the attacks. The officer should use techniques and concepts taught in the course to address the attacks. This drill will assist the officer in inoculating themselves to ambush or surprise attacks.

3-2-1 DRILL

In this drill, one partner will attack and freeze for 3 seconds. In those three seconds the other partner should counter and attack in a spontaneous fashion. At the end of the three seconds the attacking partner will then break away and attack again. The purpose of this drill is to allow the officer to acquire target acquisition skills, proper coordination, attack sequencing and timing. Once the officer feels comfortable with 3 seconds, the drill should drop down to 2 seconds, and finally one second. This progression will lead the officer to real time sparring and scenarios by gradually building the skill level needed for a more realistic tempo in training.

IMPAIRMENT DRILLS

Officers should all learn what it is like to have to defend themselves regardless of how they may be impaired by injury, lighting conditions, terrain, etc. Impairment drills should be used to simulate these various conditions. Some ways of achieving the simulation include:

-Vision Impairment: Rub lip balm on the protective eye wear of the officer. This will simulate partial or complete impairment of vision. Low light, strobe lights and other methods can also be used.

-Dizziness: Officers may feel dizzy from blood loss, head injuries, etc. To simulate this officers can simply spin, guided by a partner.

-Distracting Audio: Loud music, sirens, horns etc can be used in the training session to simulate realistic chaotic sounds

QUICK BLOCK DRILL

In this drill the officers should partner up and feed each other random angles of attack. The other officer should use the blocking techniques in a random, free flow form to build the attributes related to the skill.

CHAPTER SEVENTEEN

WARRIOR PHILOSOPHY AND THE WINNING MIND-SET

"Weakness of attitude becomes weakness of character"

Albert Einstein

"First know yourself, and then know others. Continually polish your mind." Gichin Funakoshi

Without the proper philosophy and a warrior winning mind-set the techniques and tactics will not be as effective as they should be in a physical confrontation. The winning mind-set is essential for anyone who desires to live their lives as warriors. What does it mean to live the way of the warrior? There has always been a debate whether one is born with the warrior personality or whether one can develop this mind-set. Many of the special force units like the Army Rangers, Green Berets, Marine Recon and Navy SEALS believe one has to already have the "never give up warrior mind-set" personality to succeed in those units. On the other hand are those who believe those warrior traits can be developed through training. I suspect both points of view can show examples to back up their positions. The truth may be somewhere in the middle.

I have always believed the mind is the most deadly weapon. The ability to endure and keep going when your body is exhausted is not just a physical test, but more importantly, it shows that the mind controls the body in true warriors. The majority of people allow their physical exhaustion to rule their mind, where the person with a warrior mind-set will refuse to be limited by just physical discomfort. Every warrior society recognized the simple fact, that by pushing the body to its limit, a mental toughness develops at the same time. This is the reason so few individuals make it into special force units of the military.

From my experience with law enforcement officers and martial artists, there are certain personality traits that foster and nurture the warrior spirit. Most serious athletes in contact type of sports also have a winning mind-set, which is part of the warrior personality. However, the difference between what I call the warrior mind-set and just the winning mind-set is the way individuals manage their entire lifestyle. For example, some individuals who were great athletes quit working out and fail to improve themselves when they stop playing the game. Real warriors try to maintain a certain level of fitness and keep up their physical skills throughout their lives. I have seen this essential trait in most of the people I associate with and believe it is part of the total warrior life style.

It is true that one cannot defeat age and as we get older our physical skills will also decline. This is just a fact of life. Unfortunately, ages catches up with us no matter how hard we try to fight it. However, true warriors still attempt to improve themselves at whatever level they are at the time. Gichin Funakoshi, the founder of Shotokan Karate, even in his 80s would begin practicing karate every morning before his morning tea. Even at his advanced age he would strike the Makiwara board thousands of times a day. Being a warrior is not just about lifting weights a few days a week at the gym. It is more about making a lifetime commitment to hard physical and intellectual training all of your life.

This is not an easy task, but for the warrior, it is the only way to live. This is why I do not believe everyone is cut out to "live the way of the warrior." Warriors do not allow the disease of laziness to control them. Warriors are many times thought of as fanatics because of the single-minded dedication to the ideals and philosophy of the warrior. Warriors keep their physical and weapon skills up in order to be prepared for combat, whether it comes or not.

Quite simply, warriors make training a priority in their lives. They will find a way to train no matter how busy they may be in their jobs. While working as a full time police officer and I also worked several extra jobs at the same time in order to provide more for my family. Nevertheless, I still worked out at least five days a week. Rather than eat lunch, I would work out during that time. I would work out before my shift or after my shift. Some called me an obsessive compulsive person, and that may be true, but I felt it was merely the price I had to pay for living the way of the warrior.

Even in my advanced age (73) and with all my medical issues I still work out every day for an hour in the pool practicing all my martial arts and other combat exercises in order to at least maintain a fair level of physical fitness and skill.

In conclusion, living the way of the warrior is not a lifestyle for everyone. Only those who are willing to forge their mind, body and spirit in a cause bigger than themselves can enter the warrior's domain. A warrior is a predator hunter and a protector of the weak, the meek, the injured and the disabled. They are people willing to walk in harm's way to help protect people from the predators in the world. They include the firefighters who climb into burning buildings to save lives. They are our brave troops who patrol the dangerous streets in foreign lands for the cause of freedom. They are the officers who work our streets every day fighting crime.

This book is dedicated to the spirit, honor and philosophy of the warrior.

CONCLUSION

Like any physical skill, class room time alone is seldom enough to reinforce the techniques and tactics so that they become automatic responses. One should review the material learned at least once a week to maintain an effective level of skill in these techniques.

It is sincerely hoped this manual will serve as a guide to the use of the straight baton for law enforcement, security and anyone who is interested in the use of the baton/stick as a self-defense tool. This book includes a lot of material and as I have stated in other physical skills volumes, a text alone cannot make you skillful. Only a combination of actual hands on training with an instructor and studying the material in the text book will produce effective results.

This book was not written to be the last word in the use of the straight baton. I strongly urge you to seek out and study as many different combat arts and weapons to increase the sum total of your knowledge.

Keep training, keep learning, and keep alert and vigilant at all times. Develop your warrior spirit every way possible.

LIVE BUSHIDO

REFERENCES AND RESOURCES

The Police Yawara Stick Techniques by Joseph J. Truncale and Gregory J. Connor, University of Illinois Press: First and Second editions.

The Pro-Systems, Bushi Satori Ryu Mini-Baton Basic, and Instructor Certification Course Manual by Joseph J. Truncale.

The Bushi Satori Ryu Official Jujitsu System manual by Joseph J. Truncale.

Persuader Defense Systems by Joseph J. Truncale. Pro-Systems. Pub.

The Use of the Expandable Baton by Joseph J. Truncale. Pro-Systems Pub

Use of the Monadnock Straight Baton by Joseph J. Truncale

Hanbo-Jutsu: An official manual of Bushi Satori Ryu by Joseph J. Truncale

The Monadnock Defensive Tactics System by Joseph J. Truncale and Terry Smith. Monadnock Lifetime Products, Inc.

Martial Art Myths by Joseph J. Truncale

Advanced PR-24 Baton Techniques by Joseph J. Truncale

The Persuader Baton by Eric Chambers and revised by Joseph J. Truncale. Monadnock Lifetime Products, Inc.

Basic Knife Handling and Knife Defense Manual by Joseph J. Truncale. Pro-Systems Publication.

Way of the Raven: Blade Combatives Volume one and Volume two by Fernan Vargas

Raven Method of Telescopic Baton by Fernan Vargas

Pro-Systems Practical Combatives Vol. 1, 2.

Larry Smith's Official Manual on Control Holds Instructor Course.

How to Use the Yawara Stick for Police by Professor Frank A. Matsuyama.

Chicago Police Department Training Bulletin on the Use of the Yawara Stick by Stanley R. Sarberneck and Charles V. Gruzanski

ABOUT THE AUTHORS

Joseph J. Truncale has been a lifetime student of the martial arts, beginning with wrestling and boxing in 1956. In 1959 he joined the U.S. Navy. In 1961, he began training in Judo and Karate while stationed in Japan aboard the USS Oklahoma City. He continued his training in Judo and Karate while in the Navy until his honorable discharge in November 1963. He sought out more martial art training, joining a Shotokan Karate club, where Mr. Sugiyama, Sensei was the chief instructor.

In 1965, he joined the Glenview, Illinois Police Department and studied Judo at the Glenview Judo club at that time. He also continued his Shotokan karate training under Mr. Copland, Sensei, who was also a student of Mr. Sugiyama, Sensei. When Mr. Copland moved from the area, Mr. Truncale continued his training under Mr. Loren Rogers, Sensei, who was also a student of Mr. Sugiyama, Sensei. At that time, Mr. Truncale attended numerous law enforcement arrest and control courses, becoming a certified instructor in many police systems. He also had intense training with other Police D.T. Instructors in Krav Maga at the Illinois State Police Academy at that time. He has been involved in the martial arts for more than 40 years, studying many combat and weapon systems under numerous excellent and well-known instructors. He has earned black belts in Jujitsu (9th Dan USMA), Karate (Shotokan style 6th Dan), Judo (5th Dan) and Kobudo (martial arts weapons). He has also studied the Yang style Tai Chi for many years with Laurie Manning, learning the 24 form, the 12 form, the Shaolin Fan form and the Tai Chi Sword form. Sifu Manning awarded him official teacher certification in tai chi.

In 1973, Mr. Truncale founded the first karate club in Glenview, teaching at the Glenview Playdium and the Glenview Park district. He also founded the first Jujitsu club at the Glenview Naval Air Station around 1980 and the first Jujitsu program at the Glencoe park district at that time.

Mr. Truncale has worked in many areas of law enforcement, but his special expertise is in police defensive tactics and police weapon fields. He has designed numerous police survival courses and has taught police and security officers from all over the world at international seminars. He is a certified International Instructor in the PR-24 Police Baton, the MEB (Monadnock Exp. Straight Baton), the Monadnock Defensive Tactics System, (MDTS), and is the Chief instructor of the Pro-Systems Mini-Baton(Persuader, Kubaton, etc.). He is also a certified Master Instructor in the CLAMP, GRASP, and OC Spray. He has had the honor to have studied under the most talented martial artists and police instructors in the world. He is the founder (Soke) of Bushi Satori Ryu, a jujitsu style that blends the traditional Samurai arts with modern combat methods. His system includes the study of 16 martial art weapons and 12 police weapons.

He has also created Samurai Aerobics, Persuader Defense System, the Mini-Baton System and Pro-Systems Practical Combatives. He has more than 2000 papers (articles, essays, reviews, poems) and more than 50 books/manuals published. He also writes several columns and has had his own newsletter called Warrior Way Reviews Newsletter. He is one of the founding directors of ASLET and has been on the advisory board of several associations such as ILEETA and IPITA. He has taught for many years at Oakton Community College and the Lattof YMCA, teaching police tactics, Jujitsu, Karate, Tai Chi, Samurai Aerobics and boxing aerobics. He has also taught numerous women's self-defense classes. He still teaches Seated Tai Chi and writes reviews on Amazon.

■■■

Fernan Vargas

Mr. Vargas holds a Bachelors of Arts from Northeastern Illinois University. Mr. Vargas also holds the designation of Violence Prevention Specialist from the National Association of Safety Professionals.

Mr. Fernan Vargas is an industry recognized trainer who specializes in Defensive Tactics, Combatives, Modern Weaponry and Combat Martial Arts. He is founder of Raven Tactical International through which he teaches Law Enforcement Defensive Tactics. Mr. Vargas also teaches Combat Martial Arts through the Military Hapkido Institute and Kuntao Chicago.

Fernan Vargas is a current Safety Patrol Leader and Trainer for the Chicago Chapter of the Guardian Angels Safety Patrol where he has worked on several high profile anti-crime campaigns. Mr. Vargas is the founder of the official Guardian Angels Defensive Tactics System. A program used to teach Guardian Angels and the public alike. With the Guardian Angels Mr. Vargas has created www.GuardianAngelsTraining.org as a clearing house for training materials used by the organization. Mr. Vargas and the Guardian Angels have demonstrated the Guardian Angels Defensive Tactics System for various television stations including WGN Chicago, Telemundo, ABC Chicago, WCIU Chicago, and NBC Chicago

As a certified Law Enforcement Defensive Tactics Instructor, Mr. Vargas has taught defensive tactics to law enforcement officers at the local, state, and federal level, as well as security officers, military personnel and private citizens from around the United States and foreign nations such as Canada, Italy and Spain. Mr. Vargas has developed programs which have been approved by the Police officer training and Standards Board of several states, and adopted by agencies such as the Pentagon Force protection Agency. Additionally, organizations such as the Fraternal Order of Law Enforcement and the International Academy of Executive Protection Agents have given formal endorsements of the programs developed by Mr. Vargas and Raven Tactical International.

Mr. Vargas has been an instructor at the prestigious International Law Enforcement Educators & Trainers Association International Conference (ILEETA). Mr. Vargas has also taught at several other Leading Industry events such as the International

Combatives Self Defense Association Conference, and the Saratoga Martial Arts Festival.

Mr. Vargas' has authored several books and his writings have appeared in numerous Industry periodicals such as The Martialist, Combat Warrior Magazine, Combat Survival Magazine, Muay Thaimes Magazine, Martial Arts Masters Magazine, Shinobi Nomo Magazine, The Defender, and Tae Kwon Do Times. Mr. Vargas has also written several books including Way of the Raven Blade Combatives, and the Tactical Jujitsu Training Series.

Currently Mr. Vargas holds over twenty instructor credentials in Law Enforcement Defensive Tactics, Edged Weapons, Impact Weapons, OC Spray, Firearms, Military Combatives Combat Martial Arts, and other related disciplines. Mr. Vargas was named Trainer of the year 2011 by the Alliance of Guardian Angels and has been inducted in several halls of fame for his instruction of Defensive Tactics and Combatives. Mr. Vargas has been inducted into several Martial Arts Halls of Fame and has been awarded the Presidential Service Award and the Shinja Buke Ryu Humanitarian Award for service to the community.

BOOKS, MANUALS, AND GUIDES
BY

JOSEPH J. TRUNCALE

1. PR-24 Police Baton Techniques: Basic and Advanced Techniques: (Co-author: with Connors Univ. of IL Press)

2. Police Yawara Stick Techniques: (Co-author: with Connors Univ. of IL)

3. Advanced PR-24 Baton Techniques: Monadnock Lifetime Products, Inc.

4. Use of the Straight Baton: Monadnock Lifetime Products, Inc

5. The Monadnock Defensive Tactics System: (Co-Author Smith) Monadnock

6. The Persuader Baton(Revised original text by Eric Chambers) Monadnock

7. Mechanics of Arrest and Control: For Law Enforcement. Rational Press

8. The Rational Approach to Arrest and Control: Rational Press

9. The Persuader Defense Systems Manual: Pro-Systems Publishing

10. Basic Handbook of Hypnosis for Law Enforcement: Pro-Systems

11. Rational Self-Hypnosis for Police Officers: Pro-Systems

12. Rational Self-Hypnosis for Everyone: Pro-Systems

13. Use of the Key Chain Holder for Self-Defense: (Co-author)

14. The Pro-Systems Official Weapon Retention Manual: Pro-Systems

15. Use of the Pepper Spray for Self-Defense Basic Manual: Pro-Systems

16. The FIST(Fast-Intense-Strong-Techniques)System of Self-Defense:

17. Season of the Warrior: A Poetic Tribute to Warriors: Author House Pub.

18. A Quick Course Guide to Women's Self-Defense: Pro-Systems

19. A Quick Course Guide to the Use of the Persuader Baton: Pro-Systems

20. A Quick Course Guide to Total Physical Fitness: Pro-Systems

21. Use of the Scientific Method & Pseudoscience: A Quick Course Guide.

22. A Quick Course Guide to Writing for Publication: Pro-Systems

23. A Quick Course Guide to Great Books of Civilization: Pro-Systems

24. A Quick Course Guide to Elements of Officer Survival: Pro-Systems

25. Facts and Fallacies in Police Defensive Tactics Manual: Pro-Systems

26. Truth and Fiction in the Martial Arts and Self-Defense: Pro-Systems

27. Common Myths about Women's Self-Defense: Pro-Systems

28. A Basic Guide to Defending Against Chokes: Pro-Systems

29. A Poetic Tribute to Warriors: Poems and Essay Collection: Pro-Systems

30. A Tribute to Warriors: A Haiku Collection: Pro-Systems

31. Nothing Ever Happens in Glenview: A Poem Collection: Pro-Systems

32. The Bushi Satori Ryu Official Student and Instructor Manual: Pro-Systems

33. The Bushi Satori Ryu Official 15 Weapons Basic Outline Manual: Pro-Sys

34. Knife Handling and Knife Defense Manual: Pro-Systems

35. Use of the Knife for Women's Self-Defense basic manual: Pro-Systems

36. Samurai Aerobics Official Basic Manual: Pro-Systems

37. Basic Use of the Cane Summary Review Manual: Pro-Systems

38. Basic Use of the Cane for Self-Defense Manual: Pro-Systems

39. The Mighty Pen: Your Self-Defense Friend Self-Defense Manual: Pro-Systems

40. The Pro-Systems 3-4 and 6-4 Basic Knife System Manual: Pro-Systems

41. The Bushi Satori Ryu Official Tanto Jutsu Basic Manual: Pro-Systems

42. The Revised (10 Angle System) Law Enforcement Knife Handling and Knife Defense Manual for the official course. Pro-Systems.

43. The Shotokan Karate Self-Defense Manual: Practical Combat Karate.

44. Karate's Multiple Strikes for Self-Defense: Karate's Forgotten Deadly Techniques: Pro-Bushi Publishing (Pro-Systems & Bushi Satori)

45. The Pro-Systems and Bushi Satori Ryu Wakizashi Basic Student Manual

46. Walking With Warriors: The Best of the Street Warrior.

47. Never Trust a Politician: A Critical Review of Politics and Politicians Publisher E-Book Time, LLC March 2008 ISBN NO. 978-1-59824-789-3

48. Baton Reverse Grip System (BRGS) Official Student Manual.

49. Pro-Systems Combatives (PSC) System: Fundamentals and Principles. Official Student Manual. Pro-Bushi Publishing.   ISBN Number: 978-0-9815405-1-1

50. Pro-Systems Combatives (PSC) System: Advanced Techniques and Concepts Official Manual. Vol. 2. Pro-Bushi Publishing   ISBN: 978-0-9815405-0-4

51. Mini-Baton Instructor Course Official Manual Pro-Systems Published in 2004.

52. Martial Arts Myths: Fact and Fallacy about the Martial arts and Law Enforcement: Order from Café Press Publisher. ISBN: 1-892686-11-2

53. Hanbo-Jutsu: Use of the Hanbo, Cane, Walking Stick and Baton for   Self-Defense. Pro-Bushi Publishing.

54. The Mighty Pen: Use of the Pen as a Tactical Self-Defense Tool. Pro-Bushi Publishing:

55. Haiku Moments: How to write, read and enjoy Haiku.   Publisher: Publish America. ISBN: 978-1-4512-9364-7 Softcover   978-1-4512-9363-0 Hardcover Order the above book from   www.publishamerica

56. Predator Hunter: A Warrior's Memoir Publisher: Publish America Order from www.publishamerica ISBN: 978-1-4560-1108-6

57. Karate Combatives: Reality-Based Karate for the Street (Vol. 1)   Pro-Bushi Publishing: ISBN: 978-0-9815405-3-5

58. Weapons of Karate Combatives: Karate Combatives (Vol. 2) Pro-Bushi

59. Seated Zen Karate: A Pro-Bushi Basic Manual.

60. Tactical Principles of the most effective combative systems (Revising at this time).

61. A Poetic Tribute to Autumn: The most beautiful time of the year. (PBP)

62. Haiku for special occasions (A Pro-Bushi publication)

63. Short Cat Poems: A poetic tribute to cats (A Pro-Bushi publication)

64. Pro-Systems Complete Straight Baton Manual for Law Enforcement and security officers Co-Author Fernan Vargas

SPECIAL THANKS

Many people have assisted me over the years in getting my books and manuals published. I would like to give special thanks to them. To my loyal students who have helped me with the photographs and the editing of this text. Thank you Timm McIntyre, Joe Mrowiec, Michael, Ryan and Joe Fry.

I want to give a special thanks to my friend and fellow martial artist, Fernan Vargas, for his encouragement and help in getting this manual out to the general public. Without his assistance I would not have revised this manual for publication.

I have had the honor and pleasure to have been trained and taught by some of the best minds in the martial arts and law enforcement. In my previous texts, I have attempted to name all these wonderful people, but the list keeps growing as I learn from more instructors. After all, learning is a lifetime activity. I would like to give special thanks to the numerous martial art and law enforcement instructors who have shared their knowledge and techniques with me. Whether it was one or a thousand techniques, I THANK YOU.

CPSIA information can be obtained
at www.ICGtesting.com
Printed in the USA
BVOW07s2154040318

509330BV00022B/55/P